Astral Projection for Beginners

Descriptions, Instructions, History and Classification

Contact: www.HarryEilenstein.de
Harry.Eilenstein@web.de
Harry Eilenstein at youtube

Production and publishing: BoD - Books on Demand, Norderstedt

ISBN: 9783753454276

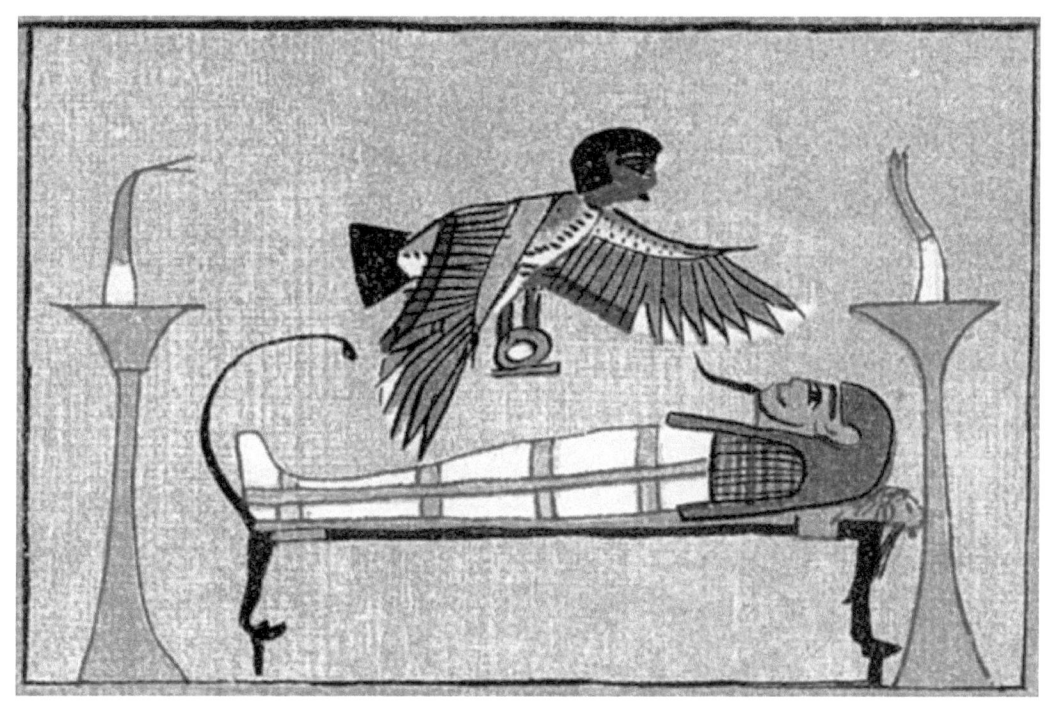

the laid out corpse of Ani
with his astral body floating above him ("Ba" = soul bird),
on the left and on the right each an incense stand

Papyrus of Ani, Egypt, 1240 B.C.

Table of contents

I What is Astral Projection?

I 1. Astral projection

Astral projection is one of the central experiences in magic and religion. It is so out of the ordinary that, although it can be described, it cannot be grasped in words, but must be experienced.

Astral projection is ultimately something very simple: one is outside of one's own physical body with one's consciousness and with one's ability to perceive.

One is so used to the fact that the consciousness is in the body and that the ability to perceive is bound to the physical sense organs that such an astral projection is difficult to imagine if one has not already experienced it.

On an astral projection one sees one's own body from the outside – e.g. lying 2m below oneself, while one is floating above it. One can also move away from one's physical body with one's consciousness and ability to perceive. One can go to any place and look at and hear everything there – without taking one's own physical body with him.

I 2. Distinction from other terms

There are a lot of similar terms to "astral projection", some of which have different meanings, and also some phenomena that are closely related to astral projection. These phenomena and terms can be distinguished from each other as follows:

Astral body: This term comes from the physician Paracelsus and literally means "star body", by which is meant "body of stars", i.e. "the body coming from the sky". "Astral body" thus refers to the soul that comes to this world from the otherworld at birth and returns to the otherworld at death. Terms like "star-body" are also found among the Egyptians and other early cultures – they refer to the fact that the stars in the night sky were thought to be the souls of the dead.

Ecstasy: This term means "going out", which originally meant leaving the physical body with the astral body. Today, this term is most often used in the sense of "altered state of consciousness through oneness."

Otherworld journey: The souls (astral bodies) of the dead are in the beyond. Consequently one can understand also each contact with the souls of the ancestors as an otherworld journey. However, whether it is really an astral journey or simply a telepathic contact with the ancestors, as for example in the systemic family constellations, must be checked in each individual case.

Trance: This word, like the prefix "trans-" which is widely used today, has the meaning "across". Originally, the word "trance" meant an astral projection, i.e. a crossing over into another realm, by which the beyond is meant. Nowadays, however, this term is used rather imprecisely for many different "unusual" states of consciousness.

Exomatosis: This is a term coined by the Cypriot healer and magician Daskalos. It roughly means "going out" and is identical to "astral projection".

"Out of body" experience: This is a widely used term in English literature for the experience of the astral projection. The practical thing about this term is that it describes the experience itself very directly: "out of body". So this term is a variant to "trance" and "ecstasy".

Dissociation: In psychology it is generally assumed that astral projection has no real basis, but is a form of hallucination – but this explanation does not explain the possibilities of perception during astral projection. The term itself means "separation", which does not mean astral projection, but only the separation of a part of the psyche, a splitting of the psyche, a pathological distancing from one's own body, and so on.

Etheric journey: One finds in some texts (especially among the Rosicrucians, Freemasons, Theosophists and Antroposophists) a complex system describing various aspects of the non-physical body by which one can leave one's physical body. In these texts, the astral body is usually associated with the emotions, the etheric body with the life force, and the mental body with the mind. Accordingly, in these texts there is an astral journey, an etheric journey, a mental journey, etc. - depending on the part of the non-physical body with which one leaves the physical body.

Flight dream: The experience of flying in nocturnal dreams mostly goes back to the fact that one leaves the physical body a little bit with the astral body during sleep. This happens unconsciously, of course, as one sleeps.

Dream journey: The dream journey is not an astral projection, but a "conscious dream". In this state the waking consciousness and the subconsciousness (dream consciousness) are coordinated with each other – so one can dream consciously. Since telepathy is the perceptual form of the subconscious mind, it is much easier to perceive telepathically on a dream journey than in the normal waking state.

Shamanic journey: Originally, a shamanic journey was an astral journey – one becomes a shaman by experiencing an astral projection. However, this term is now mainly used for "dream journey where a steady rhythm is drummed". This monotonous drumming is a concentration aid well known by shamans.

Fantasy journey: This term is identical to "dream journey." It suggests, however, that the experiences of such a journey arise from the imagination and therefore should not be taken seriously …

Daydream: In a daydream one usually gets unintentionally from the waking consciousness into a "conscious dream", thus on a dream journey. Thereby no astral projection takes place.

Telepathy: This form of perception is always possible – it is independent of the momentary location of the astral body (in the physical body or outside). Thus, successful telepathy is no evidence of an astral projection.

Mental journey: In such a journey, one merely goes to another place in one's thoughts. If one actually restricts oneself to one's own thoughts, one also has only one's own memory and logic at one's disposal, but no direct, telepathic perception. If one begins to see pictures inwardly, it has become more than only a mental journey – the beginning of a dream journey …

Life force body: This term is an alternative to "etheric body" and "astral body" and refers to the fact that the substance of what leaves the physical body during the astral journey is called "life force". There are a large number of traditional terms for this life force, such as the Egyptian ankh, the Germanic od, or the Indian prana.

Clairvoyance: In a narrow sense, "clairvoyance" is the perception of the life force or a complete astral body (which is composed of life force) as a milky white glowing shadow with a slight blue glow.

Ghost: A ghost is the clairvoyantly perceived astral body of a dead person – usually as a whitish shadow. This type of perception of the astral body is the origin of the "bed-sheet ghost" motif.

Silver cord: This is a clairvoyantly perceived connection between a person's astral body and his physical body, leading from solar plexus to solar plexus. Such a silver cord can sometimes be perceived between relationship partners or between mother and child. They are, among other things, so to speak "telepathy cables"; also dependencies and life force vampirism runs through these connections. However, this silver cord is not perceived during every astral journey.
This "silver" is another description of the milk-white colour of the life force.

I 3.   The meaningful conceptualization

If you want the terms you use to be well grounded and to know exactly what you are talking about, it is advisable to start by looking for experiences. Then, if certain experiences or certain aspects are repeated in these experiences, one can give these experiences or aspects a name. Of course it makes sense to use already existing terms for these phenomena, if it is clearly recognizable that they designate the meant phenomenon.

If, on the other hand, one starts from concepts and tries to fill them with contents, i.e. to reproduce them intellectually or to find matching experiences, there is the danger of more or less empty terms, where one actually does not know exactly what is meant by them or whether they actually designate something really existing.

You can, of course, read and look at such concepts and then see if they inspire you to do an experiment. A good experimental instruction is worth a lot, because it brings one to an experience – and one's own experiences should be the basis of one's world view.

One should also be careful with the term "astral projection" in the way recommended here. If one has already experienced a leaving of one's own body, one knows something that can be named with this word – then one knows what is meant by the word "astral projection". If one has not yet experienced something like this, one may find instructions in books on the subject that will enable one to have such an experience – then the book has been useful.

If in the course of time with increasing experiences with astral projection it should turn out that one can observe different and clearly distinguishable phenomena, it makes sense to designate these different phenomena also with different terms.

With this procedure one keeps both feet firmly on the ground even in the case of astral projection experiences …

I 4.   The Experience of Astral Projection

As with most things, there are different variations here. However, all astral projections have in common the leaving of one's own physical body.

Some people experience themselves in a kind of second body made of a pale, misty and milk-white light, which has a slight blue glow – others experience themselves as a point of consciousness floating in the air. Thus, the perception of one's own astral body as a ghost-like second body consisting of life force does not necessarily occur.

Primarily on an astral projection the sense of sight is used (80% of the perceptions of the human being are of optical nature), but sometimes also the sense of hearing and the sense of touch come along. The sense of smell, taste or temperature sensations rarely play a role.

Another phenomenon that is reported very often is the altered optical perception. On an astral journey, for example, one is no longer dependent on light to be able to see something – one's own life force perceives the life force in other things and then translates this into optical images. These images often have something blurred, are mostly gray without colors and are somehow soft. It seems as if every room is filled with a soft, diffuse light, which makes it possible to perceive the things in this room. This kind of perception sometimes occurs on dreams and also on dream journeys and even in fantasy-literature.

When you dream that you are crawling through a cave or walking through a forest in the dark of night, you sometimes see this kind of "life force imagery" in your dream.

One can use this form of perception also in dark rooms, in deep caves or in a moonless night in the forest – this form of telepathic perception can be activated not only on an astral projection.

Probably the most famous depiction of this form of perception can be found in the movie "The Lord of the Rings": When Frodo puts on the "One Ring", he no longer sees the physical world, but the world of life force. There he can then clearly perceive the nine Ringwraiths, among others.

This ring is therefore a kind of astral projection ring, which is why it makes its wearer invisible – after all, the astral body is invisible to the physical eyes.

Originally this ring has been a symbol for the otherworld projection – among the

Germanic tribes it belonged to the elf king Alberich, who has been the sun-god and godfather Tyr in the nocturnal underworld as the god of the dead.

II   Where does astral projection occur?

The next question is where astral projection occurs, by what it can be triggered, how it can be specifically induced, and so on. Here we find quite a great variety, which is to be expected for such a fundamental experience that relates to the relationship between consciousness and the physical body – after all, structures that are close to the roots of our being should also be found in many everyday experiences.

II 1.   The spontaneous astral projection

Spontaneous astral projection is unplanned, unwanted and in some cases unconscious. It occurs quite frequently.

II 1. a)   Sleep

During sleep, the astral body detaches itself from the physical body to some extent, which can be experienced as a flight dream.

There is also the possibility to wake up in a dream and still continue dreaming – this is then an unplanned dream journey. From this state one can switch from the perception of the inner images to the perception of the outer images and perceive one's own surroundings with the eyes still closed. From there it is only a small step to astral projection, that is, to leaving one's own body.

The motionlessness of the sleeping person is an aspect of astral projection: the captain has temporarily left the ship.

II 1. b)   Fainting

One can understand a fainting as a "spontaneous sleep". In fainting, too, the astral body has left the physical body, and, as in sleep, the waking consciousness is shut off.

Fainting has two types of causes. The first type of cause is a physical impairment such as a severe blow to the head or a major blood loss; the second type of cause is an overload of the processing capacity of the waking consciousness due to a shock, a great fear, or the like – when the waking consciousness is overloaded, it shuts down … input overkill …

In case of fainting there are also two possibilities in another respect. In the first form the waking consciousness and the ability to remember ends completely at the beginning of the fainting and returns only after the end of the fainting – then mostly the classical question "Where am I?" is asked. In the second form, one remains largely conscious and experiences, for example, how the body becomes stiff and one can suddenly see oneself from the outside, but one is no longer able to move and direct one's own body – at the end of the fainting, one then returns to one's body and is able to act again.

II 1. c) Seizure

There are so-called seizures in some diseases and physical disorders. One variant of seizure is that the body of the person suddenly becomes stiff and sometimes begins to twitch, and if the person was standing before, he falls over.

Here, too, the astral body leaves the physical body. Therefore, the obvious first aid in case of an attack (besides calling an ambulance immediately!) is to place the right hand on the solar plexus and the left hand on the heart chakra. The former recalls the astral body by the silver cord, the latter helps the person to become conscious again. This first aid probably works best when the helper already has some practice in perceiving and directing the life force.

During a seizure, the astral body has suddenly left the physical body for internal physical or psychological reasons. Afterwards one should in any case have it investigated what the cause has been.

II 1. d) Anesthesia

The purpose of anesthesia is to partially or completely shut down a person's ability to perceive. Since the normal (non-telepathic) perceptive faculty is coupled to the waking consciousness, the complete shutdown of the perceptive faculty also shuts down the waking consciousness. Thus, one is put into an artificial sleep.

As in normal sleep, the waking consciousness is also shut down and the astral body leaves the physical body in the artificial sleep of anesthesia. Just as one can enter a dream of flight during sleep, one can regain waking consciousness during anesthesia – and then experience oneself as floating above oneself. In such a case, one can, for example, watch the doctors taking out the appendix of one's own body, which one is looking at from the ceiling of the room. During such an awakening from anesthesia the body sensations remains switched off – one is not in one's own body …

Such surgical astral projections have occurred frequently especially in former times, when one still anesthetized with chloroform.

II 1. e) Near-death

If one gets into a dangerous and hopeless situation, it can happen that one faints. For example, if you are unarmed and a 100m deep ravine yawns behind you and a pack of hungry lions approaches from the front, your soul may decide that there is no point in witnessing you being eaten by the lions or falling into the abyss now. Then the captain leaves the ship and you do an astral projection – in this way you see your body being eaten by the lions, but you do not feel the physical pain.

Such danger-induced or shock-induced astral projection can also occur in car accidents, a fall from a horse, rape, in the war-trenches and similar extreme situations.

If one is lucky enough to survive the dangerous situation against all expectations, the astral body returns to the physical body and one lives on. The memory of such an astral journey is generally called a "near-death experience".

These "danger/shock faints" have also been observed in animals – for example, chickens attacked by a hawk. Astral projection (and consequently the astral body) is therefore not a purely human phenomenon, but a phenomenon probably present in all animals.

II 1. f) Children's games

There are children for whom astral projection is something completely normal. If you talk to them, they tell you, for example, that they often play with their building blocks and at the same time sit on top of the cupboard and watch themselves playing on the carpet below. This version of astral projection, in which the body remains active and capable of action, also occurs in adults, but seems to be quite rare.

A similar phenomenon also occurs with children during great stress – they then suddenly watch themselves from the outside behaving in the stressful situation. This is usually called "dissociation" in psychology. As a rule, this kind of astral projection does not strike children as something special and therefore worth telling. Usually it is necessary to talk to the children often in order to get such experiences told by them.

14

II 1. g)   First attempts at meditation

It also happens that someone experiments with breathing techniques from yoga, with meditations or with ecstasy methods and suddenly leaves his own body. In such a case, one has obviously created such an upheaval in one's own life force through one's own "wild experimentation" that the astral body briefly detaches from one's own physical body.

In order to achieve such an effect, however, one must in most cases have already made quite wild experiments and mixed the most diverse methods.

II 1. h)   First Sex

Sex can also have the effect of throwing one's life force into turmoil – especially the first sexual experiences, where it can happen that a very great sexual tension builds up but cannot be discharged. In such a case, one may be very exhausted on the one hand, but on the other hand be so much "under power" that one falls asleep, but at the same time remains awake – and thus makes a fully conscious astral projection.

II 2.   The intentional astral projection

In intentional astral projection, one knows what one is doing – or at least tries to experience astral projection consciously. In many cases this happens after one has already experienced a spontaneous astral projection, which has made one curious about what one can do with such astral projection …

II 2. a)   Relaxation

Probably the best known method is deep relaxation, which "imitates" some aspects of sleep and therefore comes close to the astral projection state. This includes autogenic training, some forms of letter exercises and sometimes also resting after hard work. Astral projection can then occur semi-spontaneously.

The exact method will be explained in a later chapter.

II 2. b)   Imagination

A rather seldom used possibility is the imagination of the astral body hovering over oneself. When this imagined image of the astral body has become clear, one shifts with one's consciousness into this "image".

A second method of imagination consists in imagining very intensely a place that one knows well. Possibly one then succeeds in becoming present at this place in one's astral body. This method is also rarely mentioned and probably rarely used.

II 2. c)   Crystal Ball

The best known form of astral projection brought about by an imagination is crystal ball gazing. The crystal ball is usually a concentration aid for a dream journey: Instead of seeing images internally, one projects these images onto the crystal ball so that these images become a "spatially sharply delineated vision."

However, it is known that concentration on such a sphere often leads to astral projection. Presumably this is due to the fact that one concentrates so strongly on something outside (the crystal ball), whereby then finally also one's own astral body is drawn outside.

II 2. d) Mirror Magic

Mirror magic is a variation of crystal ball gazing: You sit in front of the mirror and look at your own reflection. If you then wave to yourself and the mirror image does not wave back, you know that you have transferred your own consciousness into your mirror image and thus are just on an astral projection in the mirror – this is a rather strange experience …

II 2. e) Meditation

Sometimes astral projections also occur in meditations – especially if one mixes different methods as a beginner or if one puts one's own life force body into an "exceptional state" by very intensive breathing exercises or the like.

II 2. f) Lucid Dreaming

One can aspire to wake up in a dream during the night. This can have four different effects:

1. One wakes up normally.
2. One wakes up in a dream and then finds oneself in a dream journey.
3. One awakens in one's astral body, which is briefly outside of one's body during sleep, and then has achieved astral projection.
4. One only half awakes, but has the idea of being awake, which possibly then leads to the fact that one believes to do something in the dream or with the astral body, but one does it in reality with his physical body – this has then a sleepwalking as a result …

II 2. g) Drugs

Drugs can cause one to enter a sleep-like or death-like state, which can result in a detachment of the astral body.

This method is obviously life-threatening: if the drugs are mixed wrongly or dosed incorrectly, one can die – then one has achieved an astral projection, but it is final, since one cannot return to one's own body.

Despite this danger, drug-induced astral projection is found in many different cultures.

II 3. Bilocation

A special effect of astral projection is the visible appearance of the astral body to a person. In most reported cases this astral body is only seen, sometimes it speaks.

This process is also called "bilocation", i.e. "being in two places at the same time", because the appearance seems quite real.

One can ask oneself what actually happens during this process. How can one recognize what that is, which one sees there?

If it is only a shadow, the process is still recognizable as an inner perception, which one has projected onto the outside – this is then a vision.

However, such visions can also become very real – as their pathological form, i.e. the hallucination, shows. The person who appears to one then seems completely real. As among other things the history of the doubting Thomas shows, such a vision/hallucination can extend also to the sense of hearing and to the sense of touch. As a rule, people may sometimes doubt what they have seen, but they consider things they can touch to be real … which is a very subjective and unfounded attitude.

Why can an apparition become so clear? There are reports (e.g., from the Cypriot healer Daskalos) that some people can make their astral body become so intense that it becomes visible to others. However, one should not take every vision of a person for an astral body or a physical bilocation – there are too many other possible explanations for such a perception or vision.

II 4. Astral projection and Kundalini

In the relaxation method, one's attention gradually shifts from one's physical body to one's astral body. You do the same when you try to awaken your kundalini. Both methods coincide in the first two-thirds of the path, which means that most people who know awakened kundalini also know astral projection – and that most people who can induce astral projection also know kundalini phenomena.

During intense relaxation there appear several phenomena: The first is Relaxion of the body; the second ist the sensation of heaviness of the body; the third is the sensation of warmth of the body; and the fourth ist the vibration of the body with a frequncy of about 6 Hz.

This vibration may grow to the sensation of a kind of swaying as if on a ship – or for example the right arms seems to move suddenly to the left and then again back, though this is impossible for there lies on's own the body. It is obvious that only the astral left arm ist moving and not the physical left arm.

The stages on the two paths to the astral projection and to the awakening of the Kundalini are as follows:

Astral projection and Kundalini awakening		
Steps	*Kundalini awakening*	
	Astral projection	*Kundalini-Erwachen*
1st step	relaxing the body	
2nd step	heaviness of the body	
3rd step	warmth of the body	
4th step	vibration of the body	
5th step	swaying of the body	circling heat in the root chakra
6th step	astral projection	rising of the Kundalini

During the astral projection the vibration is increased to a movement of the astral body as a whole – to the leaving of the physical body with the astral body.

In the awakening of Kundalini, on the other hand, the vibration is increased to an inner movement – to the rising of Kundalini.

II 5. Astral projection and Chakras

The astral body consists of the life force of a human being. The chakras are the structures in the life force, i.e. the "organs" of the astral body.

The experience of an astral projection does not necessarily lead to the perception of one's chakras, but now and then such a perception occurs.

During the awakening of the Kundalini, the experience of the chakras is much more likely, since the Kundalini rises upward through the individual chakras.

II 6. Astral Projection and Trauma

Astral projection occurs, among other things, during near-death experiences. Since traumas occur during near-death experiences or similarly violent experiences, there is also a connection between astral projection and trauma. Of course, this does not at all mean that astral projection causes traumas to form.

The process of a trauma formation is as follows:

1. In a dangerous situation, the entire system is "increased" to maximum readiness for action: lots of adrenaline is released.

2. Depending on the assessment of the dangerous situation, the person concerned now has three possibilities:

a) He fights – and wins or loses and possibly dies. In case of victory the tension dissolves again; in case of death likewise, in case of defeat it remains for the time being – as fear of death or the like.

b) He flees – in which he succeeds or fails. If he escapes successfully, the tension dissolves; if he dies on the run, likewise; if he is caught up and does not die immediately, the tension remains.

c) He sees no chance in the fight, nor in the flight. In this case, the tension also remains.

3. in these three cases there can be a standstill: in the unsuccessful fight, in the unsuccessful escape and in the surrender. In these three cases the astral body and therefore also the consciousness and the ability to perceive leaves

its own body: an astral projection. The consciousness does not consider it desirable to witness the foreseeable violent suffering of one's own body.

4. If it comes now to the death of the subject, the history is to end here ...

But if he survives, he is in the situation that he is still under maximum tension because of the survived danger of life: The tension has not been relieved by a successful fight or a successful escape – the tension and the adrenaline serve to increase the physical performance to a maximum.

5. Now there are three possibilities, what happens with this survival tension and the adrenalin in the body:

a) The subject begins to shake, howl, scream, cry or rage, thus reacting off the tension and adrenaline and returning to a state of normal tension. Then everything is fine.

b) The person is prevented by some circumstances from dissolving his stress, from releasing his tension, from using up the adrenaline. Then the state of "high tension" remains and is encapsulated and repressed. This encapsulated tension then resides in the psyche of the person concerned and becomes a "pressurized, rattling can on the shelves of the basement of the subconsciousness" of the person concerned.

This pressurized can, which contains the adrenaline-charged memory of the stressful situation, is then a trauma that puts the subject's psyche into a constant state of turmoil – especially in situations similar to the one in which the trauma arose. In such situations, the subject's actions are then guided to a greater or lesser extent by the trauma – which can lead to extremely irrational behavior.

c) The person can resolve the tension, but experiences the same dangerous situation again and again. This can lead to the fact that the tension can finally no longer be relieved – it is maintained as a precaution for the next dangerous situation. This permanent high tension then also leads to a trauma: The tension can no longer be released in a normal way.

6. If the person is lucky, his trauma is recognized and he is helped to dissolve it. This healing has three steps in most cases:

a) The trauma becomes conscious and it is looked at. This should be done carefully, piece by piece, so that the person is not overwhelmed.

b) The trauma is felt. This process should also be done gradually, so that the person is not overwhelmed by the old life-threatening feelings.

c) One recognizes and feels oneself in the situation at the age one had at that time. Then one embraces this younger version of oneself that is still in the panic state.

There is also the healing version, in which the person concerned gets back into the middle of the old deathly fear feelings, e.g. through an acting representation of the situation at that time. In this case someone is needed who is able to lead the person through these panic-laden memories in such a way that the person comes to a vividly imagined and as real felt experience of victory: he kills the bear, he drives the rapist into flight, he wins the fight, etc.

Knowing how trauma occurs and knowing how trauma is healed are not directly part of the foundation for learning astral projection, but it can be helpful in some circumstances to know these dynamics.

III   The Historical Significance of Astral projection

The importance of astral projection to the history of mankind can hardly be overestimated.

The experience of astral projection during a near-death is something that showed people that there is more than the body. This was the origin of the concept of the soul and also the origin of religion …

The levitation during the astral projection has led to the fact that the astral body has been represented worldwide as a bird, as a human being with a bird's head, as a bird with a human head, as a human being with feathers, as a human being with bird's wings (angels), and so on.

The soul bird has been represented at least since the emergence of Homo sapiens, that is, for about 100,000 years, as a staff with a bird on top.

In the late Paleolithic Age, about 50,000 years ago, these bird sticks were used to create totem poles, which essentially depict a human being with his soul bird on his shoulders. There were many variants of the totem poles in later times. They were made of wood until the beginning of the Neolithic period around 10,000 BC, and then partly of stone. These stone variants then developed into the statues of the dead, the statues of the gods, the menhirs in the stone circles and the pillars in the temples.

The experience of the astral projection with a near-death suggested the assumption that this astral body continues to exist also still after the death – thus not only then further-exists, if the concerning still survived the danger situation, but that the astral body continues to exist also then, if the person concerned actually died.

From this arose the question of where the soul birds of the dead were located – thus the "place of the souls of the dead", i.e. the otherworld, came into being.

Some people, who had experienced a near-death and thus also an astral projection, succeeded by practice to be able to repeat such an astral projection voluntarily. They were then able "as a soul bird" to travel into the otherworld to the souls of the dead and to ask them for advice and help for their descendants. These people were then the first religious-magical specialists: the shamans. Traveling to the otherworld, i.e. astral projection, was the first religious act – this then became the cult of the dead and even later spiritism and systemic family constellations.

The idea that the arrival of the dead in the otherworld corresponds to the arrival of the living in this world gave rise to the three motifs of re-procreation, re-birth and re-suckling, which are the central elements of all ancient mythologies.

From these three motifs emerged the motif of the twofold goddess: the mother of the living and the mother of the dead. There have been representations of the twofold mother goddess for at least 32,000 years, having two bodies or two upper bodies or two heads, etc., or pointing upward with the left arm and downward with the right arm, that is, to this world and to the otherworld.

The soul birds have evolved to the bird gods, to the angels, to the winged messengers of the gods, to the birds as mounts of the gods and much more.

They have also connected with the snake as the spirit of the dead in the earth to a winged dragon or a feathered snake (Quetzalcoatl), with the lion as the power animal of the shaman to the winged lion (Sphinx), with the bull as the symbol of the procreative power of the (male) dead at their re-procreation to a winged bull, etc.

Astral projection, as an experience of something non-physical, has founded religion and magic as a whole, and the astral body, in the symbol of the soul-bird, has shaped all mythology.

IV Methods

The central question, of course, is how one can willingly induce an astral projection so that one can experience it.

Hoping for a near-death experience would be a bit risky as a research method, since one does not know whether one actually survives a near-death and whether it does not become a final death – then one would know that the astral body exists, but one could no longer use this knowledge in this world …

IV 1. Starting from the waking consciousness

The astral journey can start from two states of consciousness: from the waking consciousness, which must be involved if one wants to experience the astral journey consciously, and from the dream consciousness, since one is already on an astral projection during sleep (dream consciousness).

The waking consciousness as a starting point has the advantage that one can consciously direct what one does.

IV 1. a) Relaxation

Deep relaxation is the simplest and most straightforward method. You lie down and relax – it may help to listen to some music. For example, "GTA5" by Tangerine Dream is very suitable for this – you should experiment with it to find out what is best for you: silence or music – and if music, then which one.

One can then go through all parts of the body from the feet to the head and consciously relax them.

Next, one imagines again in the same sequence that all parts of the body become heavy.

Then follows the imagination of warmth in the body.

Finally, one can imagine that the body is vibrating at about 6Hz.

Instead, one can simply concentrate on relaxation and "let oneself sink into the mattress". One should experiment a bit with how much imagination is beneficial and how much one should just let happen out of simple relaxation. The phenomena "relaxation – heaviness – warmth – vibrations" occur even without imagination, if one relaxes more and more and just lies there consciously and does not move – then one gets into a kind of "awake sleep", into a "fully conscious sleep". Possibly also the breathing changes and becomes the deep sleep breathing or seems to stop almost completely – one should then simply let this happen. These four steps always occur in this order.

The vibrating is followed by a strange phenomenon: You are lying motionless and suddenly your right leg is flapping downwards through the mattress or your right arm is twitching to the left through your own body or your hands are folding downwards through the mattress and so on. So you experience that you make impossible movements – after all, you can't move your right arm to the left through your own body. That which moves there is not the physical arm, but the astral arm, that is, the arm of the astral body, for which the physical body is, after all, no obstacle – it has briefly broken free from its coupling to the physical arm.

If one simply observes these strange phenomena and continues to relax, another strange phenomenon occurs next: one seems to rock back and forth like on a ship in a heavy swell – the astral body loosens and is no longer firmly connected to the physical body. Possibly one or the other knows this phenomenon, which occurs in a similar way when one has drunk too much alcohol and then lies in bed – which then seems to be a ship at high swell … In astral projection, however, this phenomenon is much more peaceful, organic and pleasant.

Finally it can happen that one leaves the physical body out of this swaying and rocking with the astral body. Probably one will then slip back into one's physical body quite quickly, but one then already has a first experience of astral projection and a way to repeat this experience.

With some people it happens that they experience violent feelings after a certain degree of relaxation: One has sunk so far with one's waking consciousness into one's subconsciousness (dream consciousness) that one can perceive within oneself old fears, addictions and possibly also one or another trauma – possibly also a formless fear of death that rushes in as if in great waves … after all, leaving the body is closely associated with death.

Should such phenomena occur, it is necessary first to take care of these old feelings and heal them in order to be able to learn astral projection.

IV 1. b) Letter Exercises

In the letter exercises, the principle of vibration, that is, the phenomenon of 6Hz vibration of the astral body, is used to achieve astral projection. Ultimately, therefore, the letter exercises are a method of relaxation that merely addresses a different phenomenon of relaxation:

relaxation   → heaviness
letter exercises   → vibration

There are different systems of letter exercises. The method that is helpful in this context is quite simple:

You lie down comfortably on your back, relax a little and then imagine an "A" in both soles of your feet at the same time – you can possibly also imagine it colored or see if it takes on a color by itself (the "A" is often red, for example). One hums this "A" inwardly as a continuous tone. This "A" is not audibly hummed, but only in one's own imagination, it is only imagined.

After a while one changes to an "E", then to an "I", then to an "O" and finally to a "U". Then you start again from the beginning. The duration of the individual letters is chosen intuitively, as it feels good at the moment.

This very simple method causes the body to become heavy, then warm, and finally begin to vibrate. The other phenomena are the same as in the relaxation method.

The letter exercises have the advantage of giving you something to "hold on to" – which some people find easier than just relaxing more and more without falling asleep.

IV 1. c) Kundalini

The awakening of the kundalini as a tool to learn astral projection starts from the third phenomenon that occurs when one gradually shifts one's consciousness from one's physical body to one's astral body: warmth. The awakened kundalini is eventually experienced primarily as a rising fire …

relaxation   → heaviness
kundalini   → warmth
letter exercises   → vibration

The awakening of Kundalini as a tool for learning astral projection is, however, quite a complex method, since the awakening of Kundalini is not easy for most people. For those people whose kundalini has already awakened, there is very probably the possibility to get from the movements of the kundalini (inside the body) to the movement of the astral body as a whole (outside the body), i.e. to astral projection.

However, to my knowledge, this possibility has hardly been explored and I have not experienced it myself.

IV 1. d) Dream journey

In a dream journey the astral body is in the physical body – only the waking consciousness has been coordinated with the subconsciousness (dream consciousness), so that one can perceive the contents of the subconsciousness fully conscious and can also use telepathy, which is the "organ of perception" of the subconsciousness, more sovereignly.

However, this coordination and cooperation between waking consciousness and dream consciousness is an aspect of astral projection – one is waking up conscious in one's astral body, which consists of one's life force, which is also the substance of the psyche and contains the chakras as life force organs. Thus, during the dream journey one has already reached one aspect of the astral journey – one is on the "astral plane" (if one wants to call the realm of life force that way) and perceives there. One uses one's astral body and the life force and chakras within it. This inner telepathic perception during a dream journey is an ability that is also typical for astral projection. Therefore, as far as one needs only this perception for a certain goal, a dream journey is enough.

The element that is still missing for the dream journey to become an astral journey is the leaving of the astral body.

The perception of images in a dream journey is therefore, like the heaviness of relaxation, vibration in the letter exercises and warmth in Kundalini awakening, an aspect of an astral journey. Thus, one can begin an astral journey at four different points:

relaxation	→ heaviness
kundalini	→ warmth
letter exercises	→ vibration
dream journey	→ inner perception

Which approach suits you personally the most, you have to find out by your own experiments.

From a dream journey it should be possible to intensify the perception so much that one changes from a dream journey to an astral journey. I have read about such approaches, but I have not yet experienced them myself. I can change with my consciousness into other people, plants, objects etc., but this does not seem to be an astral projection with me, because I rather send out a "probe" with whose help I can then recognize, for example, where a lost object is or which feelings are in one of the chakras of a certain person.

The the general strategy is, that evoking an aspect of astral projection is a way to astral projection. Therefore it should be possible to achieve astral projection also from dream journeys.

In the instructions in question, one imagines oneself more and more intensely and more and more vividly in a place that is well known to one – thereby one finally draws oneself in one's astral body to this place.

The phenomena of astral projection, which one can use as a way to attain astral projection, occur in a certain order when striving for astral projection:

The sequence of phenomena			
Step	*Phenomenon*	*Caused by:*	*Way to astral projection*
1st step	heaviness	feel the physical body and become calm	Relaxation
2nd step	warmth	feel the life force in the body	Kundalini
3rd step	vibration	feel the life force inside	Letter exercises
4th step	inner perception	perceive from the life force	Dream journey

This sequence suggests practicing relaxation first, then awakening the kundalini, then using letter exercises, and finally practicing the dream journey. While this would be a solid "step by step" method, it would probably also be a very slow method. Therefore, it is more advisable to experiment with the different possibilities to find out which method is best for oneself.

The classification of the inner perception in this sequence is not as clear as the sequence of the three phenomena "heavy – warm – vibrating". It can be placed in different places in this sequence.

IV 1. e) Meditation

One can understand meditations as coordination between different states of consciousness. The four individual states of consciousness are:

1. the waking consciousness, in which are the contents of consciousness that are currently needed;

2. the subconscious (dream consciousness), in which all the contents of consciousness are stored;

3. the ecstasy consciousness, in which there is only a single content of consciousness to which one is attuned; and

4. the deep sleep consciousness, which is without consciousness contents and therefore silent and empty.

The deep sleep consciousness is like a house that provides space; the subconscious is like an archive that holds all memories and perceptions; the waking consciousness is like an office that processes what is relevant to the present situation; and the ecstasy state is the spotlight of the desk lamp in that office that illuminates what is of existential importance at the moment.

Now, when two states of consciousness are brought into harmony through meditation, new, more complex states of consciousness arise. One of these two states of consciousness is always the waking consciousness, because meditation is a conscious process.

waking consciousness + dream consciousness = dream journey
waking consciousness + deep sleep consciousness = inner silence (Zen)
waking consciousness + ecstasy consciousness = one-pointedness

More than two states of consciousness can be coordinated with each other, which then are quite complex processes. They occur, among other things, during mandala meditations.

The most suitable state for astral projection is the dream journey, because you have already reached the inner vision, which is typical for astral projection.

The one-pointedness can be used in order to align oneself completely to a goal – in this case the astral projection.

The state of stillness can lead to the awareness of one's own soul, that is, to the awareness of one's own essence. This does not lead to astral projection, but it can help to dissolve a possibly existing fear of leaving one's own body.

II 1. f)   Crystal ball

Looking into a crystal ball can lead to being focused on something outside, on the crystal ball. This can have the effect that the astral body also moves outward, i.e. that one experiences an astral projection. However, as far as I know, this is not a very common effect, although it does happen.

II 1. g)   Mirror Magic

The use of a mirror to learn astral projection has already been described: One sits down in front of a large mirror, looks at one's own reflection, and imagines crossing over into the reflection with one's own consciousness. If this succeeds, one has left one's physical body with one's own consciousness, i.e. with one's own astral body. It is first of all a very strange experience to look at oneself out of a mirror …

Classically, however, the mirror, like the crystal ball, is used to create a vision, that is, to project the images of a dream journey onto an object outside. For the crystal balls this is described e.g. with the Palantir in "Lord of the Rings" – and the form of the mirror magic described here is well known to almost everyone: "Mirror, mirror on the wall, who is …"

IV 1. h)   Asking Horus and the like for help

A completely different and much more indirect (but still effective) method is to ask a soul-bird deity to help you learn astral projection. Such deities are e.g. the Egyptian Horus (falcon), the Germanic Hönir (cock) and the Greek Hermes (winged shoes and winged helmet). One can also ask the eagle of Zeus, the Garuda of Vishnu or the owl of Athena for help with this request.

It might be advisable to ask for a gentle approach in this, so that one does not learn about astral projection through a near-death experience.

In which way one comes to the astral projection with this method, one knows of course always only afterwards …

IV 1. i) Drugs

A very widespread method is the production of a near-death or a waking sleep with the help of drugs, which then cause the astral body to leave the physical body.

Within a culture where such a method has a long tradition, this method, when guided by experienced persons, is reasonably safe – but in freestyle experiments a great deal of unforeseen can happen, ranging from temporary psychosis to death.

IV 2. Starting from the dream consciousness

The second group of astral projection methods do not start from the waking consciousness, but from the subconscious. They take advantage of the fact that the subconscious, that is, the dream state, is the consciousness of the astral body.

IV 2. a) Flight dreams

Flight dreams can be perceptions of astral projection during sleep – of course, there can be flight dreams originating otherwise. By "flight dreams" we do not mean dreams of flying in an airplane, parachute jumps and similar technically supported flights in the air, but mainly dreams in which one flies oneself with the help of one's body, possibly making swimming movements with the arms.

It happens that this flying in the dreams becomes so frequent, real and normal that in the dream one wonders why one can fly just now and at some times in one's life actually believes for inexplicable reasons that flying is not possible …

When you become fully conscious in such dreams, you are first of all in a dream journey, because you are in the inner world of images, that is in your subconsciousness. In these images there is also the perception of one's own floating in the astral body during sleep. The flight dream is still a dream, but one that has the perception of flying with the astral body during sleep built into the dream images.

Thus the flight dream still lacks two things to an astral journey: 1. the attainment of the complete consciousness and 2. the directing of the perception from the inner pictures to the concrete, real environment.

Since in a flight dream one is already flying and on an astral journey, there is the possibility to change from a flight dream to an astral projection – if one succeeds in becoming fully awake and directing the attention away from the inner images and to the outside. Since one is dreaming in a flight dream, one has to make the conclusion that one wants to awake in a flight dream before one falls asleep.

IV 2. b) Lucid Dreaming

A more general variant of the flight dream approach is lucid dreaming, that is, dreaming in which one has become fully awake. This is the same state of consciousness as the dreaming in the 5 seconds after waking up, in which one can still watch the last dream like a movie, like a vivid dream and like a dream journey.

However, one does not reach lucid dreaming from the waking consciousness as in a dream journey, but from the dream consciousness (subconsciousness). This "awakening in a dream", in which the dream continues undisturbed, is achieved by deciding to do this in the evening before going to sleep. A popular method is to look intensively at one of one's own hands before falling asleep and to firmly resolve to see one's own hand in the dream and then to awaken while looking at one's own hand in the dream.

Should this succeed, one is on a dream journey. From this dream journey, one can then direct one's attention outward from the inner images, with one's own hand being the gateway to this other view: one looks at one's hand in the dream, then at one's arm, then at one's body, then at the place where one is, and so on. Of course, it is possible that one still remains in the dream images – or that one simply sinks back into the dream and loses waking consciousness or simply wakes up. But lucid dreaming is one of the better known and more popular of the many ways to begin astral projection.

IV 2. c) Salt

Since astral projection is not so easy for some people, people have already developed many creative approaches.

One of them is the salt method: in the evening you swallow half a teaspoon of salt, put a glass of water on the kitchen table and before going to sleep imagine that you get up in the night and go to the glass of water and drink it because you are very thirsty because of the salt.

With the help of this method, one can succeed in waking up at night in one's astral body in front of the glass of water. However, it is also possible that one becomes a sleepwalker and wakes up with his physical body in front of the glass of water …

IV 3. Unintentional learning of astral projection

The unintentional learning of astral projection is of course the easiest, because then one does not have to learn and practice it intentionally. However, the accompanying circumstances are not always really pleasant.

IV 3. a) Play

Some children consciously leave their bodies, especially when playing or falling asleep, and then watch themselves playing or lying asleep.

Some children retain this ability throughout their lives, while a large proportion lose it at about the age of 5 years. This seems to be based on the same dynamic as the ability to remember past lives or to see the future, which also dissolves in many children at about 5 years of age.

Telepathy and thus also "temporal memory", i.e. remembering past lives or seeing the future, are tied to the astral body (subconscious, life force). Therefore, it is plausible that the ability to astral projection and temporal telepathy are lost at the same age.

Apparently, something develops in the psyche at the age of about 5 years, which hinders the simple, open and naive perception. Probably it is the from this time on clearly more contoured and structured world view, into which such experiences do not fit, at least in our culture.

The integration of astral projection into our culture would therefore probably enable many people to retain the astral projection ability from their childhood into their adulthood.

IV 3. b) Diseases

Illnesses can weaken the body so much that one finds oneself in a state between waking and sleeping, between waking consciousness and subconsciousness. In this state the astral body is also no longer as tightly bound to the physical body as usual, so that astral projection can occur more easily.

IV 3. c) Near-death experience

Learning the astral projection through a near-death experience cannot be wished upon anyone – the risk of the near-death becoming an actual death is simply too great. However, if one has experienced astral projection during a near-death, one can consciously induce astral projection by going into the memory of the astral projection experience (if the near-death has not induced the formation of a trauma).
This is the classical shamanic method.

IV 3. d) Shock

A shock can be as effective as a near-death, that is, an experience so violent that one cannot cope with it, which is why one leaves one's own body. Typical shock situations that can trigger something like this are car accidents and rape.
You cannot wish such experiences to anyone, but you can possibly use them to learn astral projection – although it may be necessary to first resolve the trauma that may have been caused by this experience.
This trauma healing is of course valuable for the whole life of the person concerned. A trauma may make it difficult in some cases to use an astral projection memory for learning intentional astral projection.

IV 3. e) Fainting

Fainting in some cases causes only partial unconsciousness. Because of this, it is possible to see oneself from the outside during a swoon, i.e., to experience astral projection. Depending on the occasion for this fainting, this astral projection memory is trauma-free and therefore well usable for learning astral projection.

IV 3. f) Poisoning

Sometimes there are poisonings in which the person suddenly finds himself outside his body. Such an experience is also not desirable, but it can be used as a connecting point for learning intentional astral projection.

IV 4. Initiations

The initiations and the mystery cults in which these initiations took place emerged simultaneously from China to the European Atlantic coast around 600 BC. Their roots go back to the Paleolithic Age.

> In the Paleolithic Age, shamans experienced astral projection through near-death and then learned to perform it willingly.

> In the Neolithic Age, the shaman-priests of the time sought hand-crafted magical ways to evoke astral projection. Fasting, dances, isolation in a cave, drugs and the like were used as aids.

> In the epoch of kingship, the Neolithic shaman-priests split into the priests, who performed the rituals of the cult, and the shamans, who performed the otherworld journeys at the funerals, at the coronations of the kings, and when asking for advice and help of the ancestors.

Around 600 B.C., the idea emerged that everyone should make an otherworld journey and thereby experience astral projection – allowing everyone to experience that they are more than just their physical body. This approach was also connected with the idea that everyone has to create his own life – one could say that there was the motto "Everyone his own king!". In order to gain the experience of astral projection and also this independence, the initiation rituals of the Mysteries were developed on the one hand and the meditations on the other hand.

The meditations were based on the otherworld journeys of the shamans – so they were originally instructions on how to experience one's astral body. These meditations consisted of imitating what happens after death – as shown, among other things, by the Tibetan Book of the Dead, which is one of the bases for the Tibetan meditations.

The mysteries were a ritually staged otherworld journey. Thereby the most different aspects of the otherworld journey could be the main motive of the ritual: the funeral fire as the gate to the otherworld (Mysteries of Eleusis, Zarathustra), the fire walk as otherworld journey (Greeks, Celts, Teutons), the cave (Persians, Celts, presumably also the Hittites), the near-drowning (Celts), etc.

The main meditation teachings and mysteries of that time were:

Wisdom teachings and mystery cults		
Country/People	Teaching	Mysteries
Chinese	Loa-tse, Dschung-tse	
Egyptians		Mysteries of Isis, Mysteries of Osiris, Cult of Serapis
Indians	Buddha, Jaina, Patanjali	Yoga, Meditation
Persian	Zoroaster	Mysteries of Mithras
Northern Mesopotamia		Cult of Cybele, Cult of Attis
Greeks	Pythagoras	Mysteries of Eleusis, Cult of Dionysus, Cult of Despoina
Thracians	Zalmoxis, Orpheus	Mysteries of Samothrace, Cult of Sabazius
Romans		Mysteries of Sol invictus, Mysteries of Liber Pater, Cult of Jupiter Dolichenus
Celts		Initiation of druids
Teutons		Initiation of warriors

Two other well-known mystery cults are the sun dances of the North American Plains Indians and the sun dances of the African peoples. In these cults, however, it is difficult to estimate the time of origin.

The widespread vision quest probably dates back to the Neolithic period – it can be seen as a more individual form of the mysteries. It is quite certainly one of the roots of the Mysteries.

One of the most rustic and probably effective methods is that of the Celts: The prospective druids were tied to a log and then plunged into a water-filled shaft until they were nearly drowned. Then they were brought out again and revived. Through this ritual induced near-death, they experienced astral projection. This was called the "triple death": 1. being tied up, 2. hanging from a tree, and 3. (almost) drowning. Imitation is not recommended …

IV 4. a)   Death representation

One aspect of the initiations is the death representation. It ranges from the symbolic death in the Mithras Mysteries to the real near-death experience in the Druid initiation among the Celts.

The more or less realistic ritual representation then evoked in many cases an astral projection experience – or in other words: the encounter with one's own soul.

IV 4. b)   Fasting

Fasting and abstaining from drinking can also evoke astral projection – as the saying goes, "Food and drink keep body and soul together." The renunciation of food and drink should therefore sooner or later detach the astral body from the phyical body – ideally already before starving or dying of thirst …

IV 4. c)   Isolation

A very similar approach is the isolation deep in a cave or similar. This method would be called a "sensory deprivation" in the technical language of psychology. This, too, can lead to eventually leaving one's body and beginning an astral journey.

IV 4. d)   Ecstasy

Ecstasy appears relatively rarely in the mystery cults – it has been partially adopted from the Semitic Attic cult into the Isis mysteries. However, ecstatic dance, self-injury, firewalking, and the like, i.e. methods of "maximum excitement" are not the norm, but the meditation, thus the death-like silence – the "maximum relaxation".

IV 4. e)   Potions containing drugs

In many mystery cults and in shamanism in general, herbal potions and herbal ointments have been used to induce a death-like state and associated astral projection. They are found, among others, in the Odin cult of the Germanic tribes, among the witches ("witches' flying ointment"), in the mysteries of Eleusis, in the rituals of the Scythians and Persians, in the Soma cult of the Indians, among the Indians of Central and South America, among the peoples of Siberia, and so on.

This is a chemical-pharmaceutical method of evoking astral projection – an intentional and ideally well-controlled intoxication.

Such a method of chemical-pharmaceutical evocation of astral projection, but not intentional, has been the commonly used anesthesia with chloroform before operations.

The dangerousness of the "astral projection plants" used in the mysteries and cults varies greatly, but all of them induce a near-death – and are therefore highly dangerous.

IV 5. Hypnosis

In hypnosis, astral projection does not normally take place, but there are still some parallels to astral projection.

In hypnosis, the hypnotist switches off the waking consciousness of the hypnotized by suggestions and puts himself in the place of the waking consciousness of the hypnotized, thus being able to direct the hypnotized by his words.

In these suggestions the following words play a great role: "You are completely relaxed … You become quite heavy … You become pleasantly warm … You are getting tired … You fall asleep …"

The first three adjectives, i.e. "relaxed", "heavy" and "warm" correspond to the first three phenomena one experiences when trying to achieve astral projection through deep relaxation. The hypnotist apparently uses the same path in hypnosis as someone who wants to detach his astral body from his physical body:

   - In learning astral projection, one shifts his attention from his physical body to his astral body, which corresponds to the subconscious mind.

   - During hypnosis, the hypnotist shifts the waking consciousness of the hypnotized toward the subconscious, which corresponds to the astral body.

While the astral traveler takes his waking consciousness with him into his astral body and consequently remains awake, the hypnotist suggests to the hypnotized that he becomes tired and falls asleep – the hypnotized changes completely into the sleep state and switches off his waking consciousness.

Thus, there are four major processes, all using the same pathway:

The path to the astral body				
Step	**Process**			
	Sleep	*Hypnosis*	*Astral Projection*	*Kundalini*
1st step	relax			
2nd step	heavy			
3rd step	warm			
4th step	tired		vibrate	
5th step	fall asleep		outer movement	inner movement
result	sleep	hypnosis	astral projection	Kundalini

V   The Individual Path

The previous chapters already show that there is a great variety of methods, even if they often contain similar elements and all refer to the same path. From this variety, everyone who wants to learn astral projection must compose his own path or develop his own method – there is no patent remedy that works for everyone …

V 1.   Tradition

The first foundation is always the tradition in which one grew up. If you grew up in South America, you will probably know the methods there; if you live in Europe, you will probably have heard of the witches' flying ointment first; in general, in Western civilization, the various relaxation methods and lucid dreaming will probably be the astral projection methods you will start with.

If the particular traditional method leads to the desired success, one will usually stay with the traditional method in question; if not, one will look around in other cultures and then begin to experiment with their procedures – provided one's own motivation to learn astral projection is great enough.

V 2.   Horoscope

The horoscope tells quite a bit about one's inclination to astral projection. Horoscopes are of course very complex, so only a few suggestions can be given here.

The beginning of the first astral journey is a leap into new territory and therefore belongs to Uranus. The Uranus in the 1st house is therefore already quite conducive.

The astral body normally sits firmly in the physical body during the phase of active waking consciousness (i.e. while one is not asleep). This firmness corresponds to Saturn. Consequently, a square between Saturn and Uranus is a good basis for spontaneous astral projection without much preparation.

A Pluto/Saturn square suggests that one is more likely to experience astral projection in situations of danger (near-death experience).

A conjunction of Moon and Uranus allows astral projection to be achieved quickly through relaxation methods (Moon).

If Neptune has a square to Uranus, one is most likely to try to achieve astral projection with drugs (Neptune).

With an aspect between Mars and Uranus, one probably prefers to use ectasy techniques to start with astral projection.

V 3. "Every Jeck is different ..."

As they say so wisely in the Rhineland, "Every Jeck is different." (A "Jeck" is a carnival-participant, a fool, a clown and so on – each of them wears a different carnival-disguise ...)

This diversity also applies to astral projection – everyone must find his own way. One can draw a map on which the different phenomena and the approaches resulting from them are marked and from which also the relationship between these different phenomena and methods can be seen. The way through this landscape to astral projection, which is best suited for oneself, must be sought, tested and found by oneself.

V 4. The Map

In essence, the map to astral projection has already been sketched in the previous chapters. However, it has not yet been presented in its entirety.

The astral projection map can be found on the next two double pages. The paths to astral projection each start on the left side and then continue on the right side.

The basic structure of the map has three parts:

1. the waking consciousness, the physical body and the trigger;

2. the seven-part path (concentrate – relax – imagine – heavy – warm – vibrate – move);

3. the dream consciousness and the astral body (astral projection + three other phenomena).

See the map on pages 46-49.

The astral projection map – part 1 (left side)				
waking consciousness, physical body: trigger	path (first half)			
	concentrate	relax	imagine	heavy
death	become still	movement ends	see smoke/fog (life force)	→
sleep	lie down	relax	thoughts turn into half-dreams	heavy
relaxation	concentrate	relax	seeing images	heavy
hypnosis	concentrate	relax	the hypnotist imagines according to his words	heavy
kundalini	concentrate	→		
letter exercises	concentrate	relax	→	heavy
children's games	astral projection for fun	→		
shock	astral projection from distress	→		
near-death experience				
ritual near death	astral projection	→		
fasting	astral projection by approaching starvation (death)	→		
fainting	forced astral projection			
crystal ball	concentrate	astral projection	→	
isolation	concentration due to lack of distraction	astral projection		

The astral projection map – part 1   (right side)

path (second half)			dream consciousness, astral body			
warm	vibrate	move	1st phenomenon	2nd phenomenon	astral projection	3rd phenomenon
heat fades	breath ends	→	see light	leaving the body	astral projection	
warm	fall into sleep	sleep	dream			
warm	vibrate	sway	→	leaving body	astral projection	telepathy, telekinesis, bilocation
warm	→	hypnosis	command astral projection in hypnosis		awaken in astral body	
heat	→		kundalini rising	chakras	-	-
				→	astral projection	
heat	vibrate	→	-			
→						
→			possibly trauma formation	→		
→						
→					Astral projection	-

47

The astral projection map – part 2 (left side)				
waking consciousness, physical body: trigger	path (first half)			
	concentrate	relax	imagine	heavy
ask Horus for help	concentration	astral projection	→	
physical disturbance	→	lack of strength	astral projection	→
disease				
meditation experiments	→	high tension	→	
first sex				
mirror	concentrate	→	imagine	astral projection
imagination				
Initiation	excitement	→	death enacting	
drugs	Ingestion	→		restriction of movement ("sleep", "death")
ecstasy	one-pointed	dance, song, or the like	→	
resolution	fall asleep	→		
resolution	fall asleep	→		
resolution	eat salt and provide glass of water	→		

The astral projection map – part 2 (right side)							
path (second half)			*dream consciousness, astral body*				
warm	*vibrate*	*move*	*1st phenomenon*	*2nd phenomenon*	*astral projection*	*3rd phenomenon*
→					astral projection	-
→					astral projection	-
→			-		astral projection	
→			lucid dreaming	waking up in a dream		
→			flight dream	wake up in flight dream		
→			astral projection	awakening in the astral body at the glas of water		

49

VI   Usage

The experience of astral projection and learning to use it at will lead to various insights and possibilities for action.

VI 1.   Cognitions

The cognitions that can be gained through astral projection are very basic and have given rise to religion, among other things, and probably also to magic.

VI 1. a)   "I am more than my body."

The most important effect of the experience of an astral journey in general is the realization that one is more than one's own physical body.

From this follows as a second step the exploration of what one can do with this non-physical body: These are above all telepathy and telekinesis, i.e. non-physical perception and non-physical action – i.e. magic.

The next question is what happens to the astral body after death – if it continues to exist, death is not the end of one's existence.

This realization has another consequence: suicides do not end one's own existence, but merely change the physical existence to a non-physical existence. This means that one cannot end one's own existence – "no exit" … there is no way to get out of the game. The statement "I don't participate anymore!" is not accepted by life.

VI 1. b)   Kundalini

There is a chance that by practicing astral projection one can also discover one's own Kundalini and experience its rising. This in turn can lead one to encounter one's own shadow, that is, one's repressed fears, addictions and pains. This can be extremely unpleasant, but it offers the possibility to heal and integrate these parts of one's being and subsequently to live a much more fulfilling life.

VI 1. c) Chakras

If one reaches an experience of the Kundalini as a side-effect of one's the astral projections, one will probably be able to discover and feel one or the other chakra in oneself afterwards. However, this is already quite a circuitous way to experience (and use) one's own chakras …

VI 2. Abilities

In magic, the abilities of perception and the abilities of action should always be developed to about the same extent – being able to see something but not being able to do anything is not a good situation, and being able to act but not knowing what situation you are in does not always lead to the desired result …

Possibilities of action also arise from astral projection, although these possibilities of action need not always have as their basis the ability to perform astral projection.

VI 2. a) Seeing far away

The astral body is, so to speak, the substance of the subconscious, whereby this substance is usually called "life force". This subconsciousness can be experienced in dreams, on dream journeys and in visions. The perceptions through the astral body are the telepathy, the actions through the astral body are the telekinesis. Both can be described as processes in the life force – though the word "life force" is used here merely to give a name to the milky white glow and to the warm/hot tactile sensation, that can be experienced during these processes, and to make it easier to talk about these phenomena.

Thus, when one is on an astral journey, telepathy and telekinesis are closer to one than in the normal waking state, which is not coupled with subconsciousness. However, it is not necessary to go on an astral journey to be able to see something telepathically in the distance – e.g. to find a lost key. A dream journey is also sufficient for this.

However, there is a fundamental difference between the key search by astral projection and the key search by telepathy: In telepathy one puts oneself in resonance with the key and sends out a "telepathic probe", so to speak, which looks for the key – in astral projection one begins to goes out oneself as a whole at the place where the

51

key is located. As a result, the perceptions during astral projection are usually clearer and more distinct – but this does not have to be the case in principle.

VI 2. b)   Seeing the future

The same is probably true for telepathic perception of the future. The pictures are probably clearer if one travels into the future with one's astral body, i.e. as a whole, and not only sends a "telepathic probe" there. But I don't know that for sure.

VI 2. c)   This world and the otherworld

The otherworld journey is the "classical application" of the astral journey: The shaman travels to the souls of deceased ancestors in the otherworld and asks them for advice and help. The shamans and the shaman-priests ("seers") also almost always use otherworld journeys to discern the future – they ask the ancestors and gods about what will happen in the future.

As, among others, the systemic family constellations show, an astral journey is not necessary for the contact with the ancestors, but one can also assume here that an astral journey brings clearer and more detailed results than the sending of a "telepathic probe" or than the telepathic receiving of messages – as, for example, by the medium in spiritualism or by one of the participants in a family constellation.

VI 2. d)   Hypnosis

The ability to perform astral projection is not a prerequisite for being able to hypnotize another person or to be hypnotized oneself. However, the experience of astral projection and the understanding of the structures and dynamics involved can facilitate hypnosis for the hypnotist.

There is also the possibility that the hypnotist (who in this context would be called a "magician") commands the hypnotized person (who in this context is usually called a "medium") to leave his body and to go with his astral body to another place. Now it is hard to say whether the medium under hypnosis actually performs astral projection or merely performs an improved form of telepathy, which is caused by the fact that the medium is not disturbed by her waking consciousness and is attuned by the magician's command.

It might also be possible that the medium awakens in his astral body outside of his physical body, i.e. in another place than where his physical body is located – this would then be another possibility to experience an astral projection.

To me this possibility seems quite plausible, but I am not aware of any such attempt that has been successfully carried out.

VI 2. e) Telekinesis

One should actually be able to perform more effective telekinesis from the astral body. However, in the reports about astral projections one mainly finds the indication of how difficult it is to make oneself known to a person in his physical body from the astral body. About attempts to do this by telekinetic throwing of objects or by telekinetic creation of sounds I don't know anything.

After all, in spiritistic séances there are all kinds of telekinetic phenomena, which are obviously attributed to the ancestors present in their astral bodies. These include knocking noises, falling objects, and sometimes materializations (for a time, chocolate bars in particular materialized).

Very similar phenomena also occur during rituals – although these phenomena are then usually attributed to spirits and gods. Of course, this is neither a big difference to the ancestor telekinesis nor to the supposed astral body telekinesis.

The exercise of telekinesis from astral projection seems to be still largely unexplored.

VI 2. f) Bilocation

The already mentioned bilocation ("presence in two places at the same time") is probably essentially a special case of astral body telepathy: A person goes in his astral body to another place to other people and creates in these people by telepathy such a strong inner image that this image overlaps with the normal perceptions of these people. This then creates a vision in the consciousness of these people, i.e. they see something outside which they cannot distinguish from a real perception. This perception can extend from the sense of sight to the sense of hearing, the sense of touch, etc. – however, purely auditory visions also occur.

In principle, such a bilocation, i.e. such a vision perceived by other people, should be possible to generate even without astral projection. However, due to the rarity of this phenomenon, which already belongs to the advanced magic, it is difficult to examine the processes taking place thereby more exactly.

Have a good flight!

English Books by Harry Eilenstein

- Living Magic (261 p.)
- The Synthesis of Physics and Magic (192 p.)
- Astral Projection for Beginners (60 p.)
- Invocations for Beginners (52 p.)
- Evocations for Beginners (62 p.)
- Auto-Movement for Beginners (60 p.)
- Elves for Beginners (56 p.)
  These books will be puplished soon:
- Telepathy for Beginners
- Telepathy for Advanced Learners
- Telekinesis for Beginners
- Life Force for Beginners
- Meditation for Beginners
- Kundalini for Beginners
- Hypnosis for Beginners
- Chakra-Magic for Beginners
- Astrology for Beginners
- Ritual Magic for Beginners
- Mandalas for Beginners
- Money Magic for Beginners
- Love Magic for Beginners
- Magic Research for Beginners
- Self-awareness for Beginners
- Symbolism of Numbers for Beginners
- Language of the Moon – for Beginners
- Magic Chant for Beginners
- Prophecy for Beginners
- Shamanism for Beginners
- Magic Objects for Beginners
- Da'ath-Magic for Beginners
- Crop Circles for Beginners
- Feng Shui for Beginners
- Magic for Beginners – Anthology I
- Magic for Beginners – Anthology II
- Magic for Beginners – Anthology III
- Magic for Beginners – Anthology IV

Bücher von Harry Eilenstein

Religion allgemein
- Die sieben Schritte des Lebens (428 S.)
- Muttergöttin und Schamanen (168 S.)
- Göbekli Tepe (472 S.)
- Die Göttin von Göbekli Tepe (144 S.)
- Totempfähle (440 S.)
- Christus (60 S.)
- Dakini (80 S.)
- Vajra (76 S.)

Ägypten
- Hathor und Re 1:   Götter und Mythen im Alten Ägypten (432 S.)
- Hathor und Re 2:   Die altägyptische Religion – Ursprünge, Kult und Magie (396 S.)
- Isis (508 S.)

Indogermanen
- Die Entwicklung der indogermanischen Religionen (700 S.)
- Wurzeln und Zweige der indogermanischen Religion (224 S.)

Germanen
- Die Götter der Germanen (87 Bände – siehe nächste Seite)
- Odin (300 S.)

Kelten
- Cernunnos (690 S.)
- Taliesin (228 S.)
- Der Kessel von Gundestrup (220 S.)
- Der Chiemsee-Kessel (76)

Psychologie
- Über die Freude (100 S.)
- Das Geheimnis des inneren Friedens (252 S.)
- Das Beziehungsmandala (52 S.)
- Gefühle und ihre Verwandlungen (404 S.)
- einsgerichtet (140 S.)
- Liebe und Eigenständigkeit (216 S.)
- Von innerer Fülle zu äußerem Gedeihen (52 S.)

Heilung
- Die Symbolik der Krankheiten (76 S.)

Kunst
- Herz des Tanzes – Tanz des Herzens (160 S.)

Drama
- König Athelstan (104 S.)

Bücher von Harry Eilenstein

„Magie für Anfänger"

- Telepathie für Anfänger (60 S.)
- Telepathie für Fortgeschrittene (52 S.)
- Telekinese für Anfänger (52 S.)
- Lebenskraft für Anfänger (60 S.)
- Meditation für Anfänger (56 S.)
- Kundalini für Anfänger (100 S.)
- Hypnose für Anfänger (56 S.)
- Auto-Movement für Anfänger (56 S.)
- Chakra-Magie für Anfänger (148 S.)
- Astralreisen für Anfänger (56 S.)
- Astrologie für Anfänger (120 S.)
- Ritual-Magie für Anfänger (56 S.)
- Mandalas für Anfänger (68 S.)
- Geldzauber für Anfänger (56 S.)
- Liebeszauber für Anfänger (52 S.)
- Invokationen für Anfänger (52 S.)
- Evokationen für Anfänger (60 S.)
- Elfen für Anfänger (56 S.)
- Magie-Forschung für Anfänger (140 S.)
- Selbsterkenntnis für Anfänger (52 S.)
- Zahlensymbolik für Anfänger (60 S.)
- Die Sprache des Mondes – für Anfänger (116 S.)
- Zaubergesänge für Anfänger (100 S.)
- Zukunftschau für Anfänger (60 S.)
- Schamanismus für Anfänger (52 S.)
- Magische Gegenstände für Anfänger (68 S.)
- Da'ath-Magie für Anfänger (64 S.)
- Kornkreise für Anfänger (348 S.)
- Feng Shui für Anfänger (96 S.)
- Magie für Anfänger – Sammelband I (696 S.)
- Magie für Anfänger – Sammelband II (664 S.)
- Magie für Anfänger – Sammelband III (580 S.)

„Traumreisen"

- Traumreisen zu Heilpflanzen (700 S.)

Magie

- Handbuch für Zauberlehrlinge (408 S.)
- Tarot (104 S.)
- Physik und Magie (184 S.)
- Die Synthese von Physik und Magie (200S.)
- Die Magie-Formel (156 S.)
- Krafttiere – Tiergöttinnen – Tiertänze (112 S.)
- Schwitzhütten (524 S.)
- Mythen und Magie der Harfe (116 S.)
- Magie heute – Berichte aus der Praxis (288 S.)

Meditation

- Der Lebenskraftkörper (230 S.)
- Die Chakren (100 S.)
- Das Chakren-System mit den Nebenchakren (296 S.)
- Organe und Chakren (64 S.)
- Die platonischen Körper in den Chakren (156 S.)
- Meditation (140 S.)
- Drachenfeuer (124 S.)
- Kundalini I (676 S.)
- Reinkarnation (156 S.)
- einsgerichtet (140 S.)

Astrologie

- Astrologie (496 S.)
- Photo-Astrologie (428 S.)
- Die astrologischen Aspekte (88 S.)
- Horoskop und Seele (120 S.)

Kabbala

- Kursus der praktischen Kabbala (150 S.)
- Eltern der Erde (450 S.)
- Blüten des Lebensbaumes:
    - Die Struktur des kabbalistischen Lebensbaumes (370 S.)
    - Der kabbalistische Lebensbaum als Forschungshilfsmittel (580 S.)
    - Der kabbalistische Lebensbaum als spirituelle Landkarte (520 S.)

Die Themen der 87 Bände der Reihe „Die Götter der Germanen"

1. Die Entwicklung der germanischen Religion
2. Lexikon der germanischen Religion
3. Der ursprüngliche Göttervater Tyr
4. Tyr in der Unterwelt: der Schmied Wieland
5. Tyr in der Unterwelt: der Riesenkönig   Teil 1
6. Tyr in der Unterwelt: der Riesenkönig   Teil 2
7. Tyr in der Unterwelt: der Zwergenkönig
8. Der Himmelswächter Heimdall
9. Der Sommergott Baldur
10. Der Meeresgott: Ägir, Hler und Njörd
11. Der Eibengott Ullr
12. Die Zwillingsgötter Alcis
13. Der neue Göttervater Odin   Teil 1
14. Der neue Göttervater Odin   Teil 2
15. Der Fruchtbarkeitsgott Freyr
16. Der Chaos-Gott Loki
17. Der Donnergott Thor
18. Der Priestergott Hönir
19. Die Göttersöhne
20. Die unbekannteren Götter
21. Die Göttermutter Frigg
22. Die Liebesgöttin: Freya und Menglöd
23. Die Erdgöttinnen
24. Die Korngöttin Sif
25. Die Apfel-Göttin Idun
26. Die Hügelgrab-Jenseitsgöttin Hel
27. Die Meeres-Jenseitsgöttin Ran
28. Die unbekannteren Jenseitsgöttinnen
29. Die unbekannteren Göttinnen
30. Die Nornen
31. Die Walküren
32. Die Zwerge
33. Der Urriese Ymir
34. Die Riesen
35. Die Riesinnen
36. Mythologische Wesen
37. Mythologische Priester und Priesterinnen
38. Sigurd/Siegfried
39. Helden und Göttersöhne
40. Die Symbolik der Vögel und Insekten
41. Die Symbolik der Schlangen, Drachen und Ungeheuer
42.a Die Symbolik der Herdentiere I
42.b Die Symbolik der Herdentiere II
43. Die Symbolik der Raubtiere
44. Die Symbolik der Wassertiere und sonstigen Tiere
45. Die Symbolik der Pflanzen
46. Die Symbolik der Farben
47. Die Symbolik der Zahlen
48. Die Symbolik von Sonne, Mond und Sternen
49.a Das Jenseits I – Das Hügelgrab
49.b Das Jenseits II – Der Jenseitsweg
50. Seelenvogel, Utiseta und Einweihung
51. Wiederzeugung und Wiedergeburt
52. Elemente der Kosmologie
53. Der Weltenbaum
54. Die Symbolik der Himmelsrichtungen und der Jahreszeiten
55.a Mythologische Motive I
55.b Mythologische Motive II
56. Der Tempel
57. Die Einrichtung des Tempels
58. Priesterin – Seherin – Zauberin – Hexe
59. Priester – Seher – Zauberer
60. Rituelle Kleidung und Schmuck
61. Skalden und Skaldinnen
62 Kriegerinnen und Ekstase-Krieger
63. Die Symbolik der Körperteile
64.a Magie und Ritual I
64.b Magie und Ritual II
64.c Magie und Ritual III
65. Gestaltwandlungen
66.a Magische Angriffs-Waffen
66.b Magische Verteidigungs-Waffen
67. Magische Werkzeuge und Gegenstände
68. Zaubersprüche
69. Göttermet
70. Zaubertränke
71. Träume, Omen und Orakel
72. Runen
73. Sozial-religiöse Rituale
74. Weisheiten und Sprichworte
75. Kenningar
76. Rätsel
77. Die vollständige Edda des Snorri Sturluson
78. Frühe Skaldenlieder
79.a Mythologische Sagas I
79.b Mythologische Sagas II
80. Hymnen an die germanischen Götter